I0801742

discovermore
Your Government

The Legislative Branch

Ezra E. Knopp

Britannica Educational Publishing
IN ASSOCIATION WITH
THE ROSEN PUBLISHING GROUP

Published in 2024 by Britannica Educational Publishing (a trademark of Encyclopædia Britannica, Inc.) in association with
The Rosen Publishing Group, Inc.
2544 Clinton Street, Buffalo, NY 14224

Distributed exclusively by Rosen Publishing.
To see additional Britannica Educational Publishing titles, go to rosenpublishing.com.

Editor: Caitie McAneney
Book Design: Rachel Rising

Photo Credits: Cover; (series background) Dai Yim/Shutterstock.com; Cover, S.Borisov/Shutterstock.com; p. 4 lunamarina/Shutterstock.com; p. 5 VectorMine/Shutterstock.com; p. 6 eurobanks/Shutterstock.com; p. 7 larry1235/Shutterstock.com; p. 8 Everett Collection/Shutterstock.com; p. 9 f11photo/Shuttestock.com; p. 10 Maria Dryfhout/Shutterstock.com; p. 11 Rawpixel.com/Shutterstock.com; p. 12 https://commons.wikimedia.org/wiki/File:Nancy_Pelosi_(16526886414).jpg; p. 13 BiksuTong/Shutterstock.com; pp. 15, 16 mark reinstein/Shutterstock.com; p. 15 Ron Adar/Shutterstock.com; p. 17 https://commons.wikimedia.org/wiki/File:Social_distancing_in_the_House_Chamber_today.jpg; p. 18 trekandshoot/Shutterstock.com; p. 19 https://commons.wikimedia.org/wiki/File:Joe_Biden_signs_a_bill.jpg; p. 20 Bumble Dee/Shutterstock.com; p. 21 https://commons.wikimedia.org/wiki/File:British_and_U._S._Troops_Landing_at_Gela_Sicily.jpg; p. 22 BPTU/Shutterstock.com; p. 23 Margaret.Wiktor/Shutterstock.com; p. 24 Orhan Cam/Shutterstock.com; p. 25 New Africa/Shutterstock.com; p. 26 iama_sing/Shutterstock.com; p. 27 Avigator Fortuner/Shutterstock.com; p. 28 Jana Shea/Shutterstock.com; p. 29 PJiiiJane/Shutterstock.com.

Cataloguing-in-Publication Data

Names: Knopp, Ezra E.
Title: The legislative branch / Ezra E. Knopp.
Description: New York : Britannica Educational Publishing, in Association with Rosen Educational Services. 2024. | Series: Discover more: your government | Includes glossary and index.
Identifiers: ISBN 9781642829020 (library bound) | ISBN 9781642829013 (pbk) | ISBN 9781642829037 (ebook)
Subjects: LCSH: United States. Congress--Juvenile literature.
Classification: LCC JK1025.K66 2024 | DDC 328.73–dc23 t

Manufactured in the United States of America

CPSIA Compliance Information: Batch #CSBRIT24. For further information contact Rosen Publishing at 1-800-237-9932.

Contents

One Government, Three Parts

The U.S. government is made up of three parts, called branches. Each part has a role, or job. Power is balanced between the branches, and each one can check on the others.

The **legislative** branch is made up of lawmakers. In addition to making laws, this branch can also declare war and decide if a person the president chooses for a government job is the right fit. The legislative branch is also called Congress. It's made up of two houses: the Senate and the House of Representatives, or the House. Both groups meet at the U.S. Capitol Building in Washington, D.C.

The House of Representatives and Senate have their own parts of the U.S. Capitol Building, called chambers.

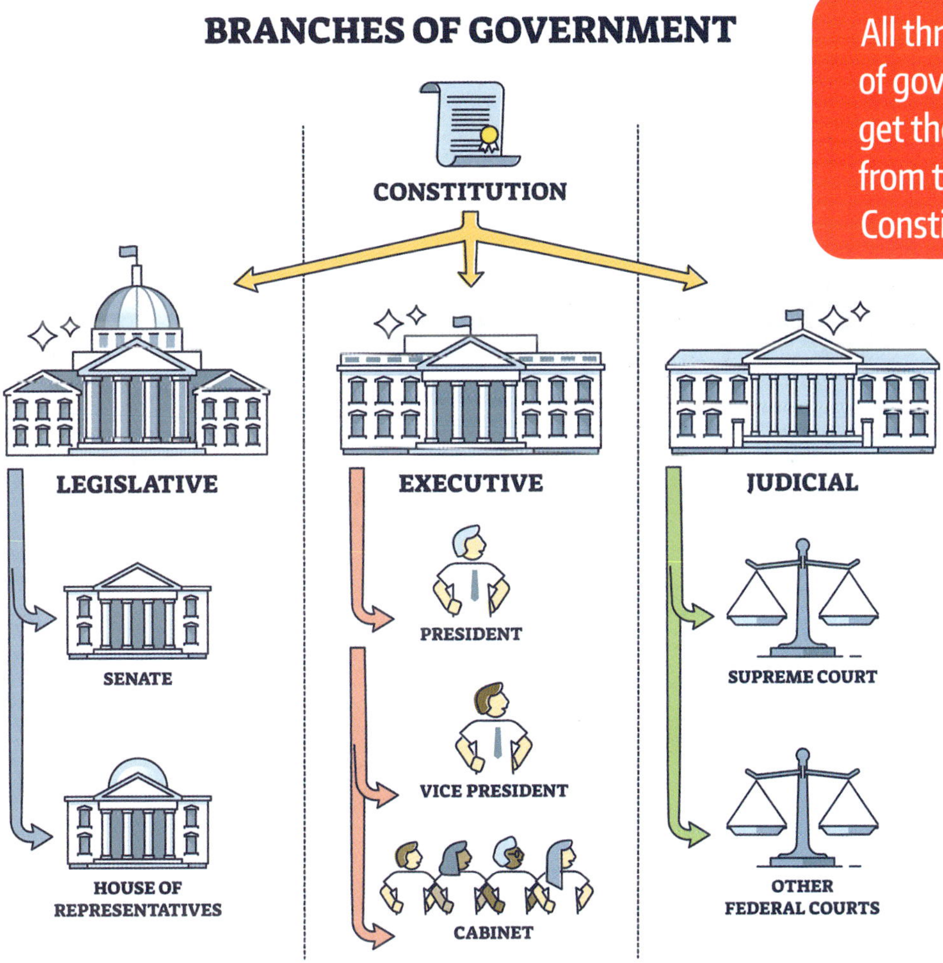

All three branches of government get their powers from the U.S. Constitution.

Lawmakers are elected as representatives of the American people, so it's their job to make sure the government is working for its citizens. Let's learn more about the legislative branch!

WORD WISE

Legislative means having the power to make laws.

Besides the legislative branch, the U.S. government also has an executive branch and judicial branch. The Constitution gives them powers too. The legislators create and vote on a bill, or proposed law. Then, the president might sign the bill into law.

The judicial branch includes the Supreme Court and other courts. All three branches of government check each other to make sure no one branch uses more power than it should.

The original U.S. Constitution can be viewed at the National Archives in Washington, D.C.

The legislative branch is set up in Article I of the U.S. Constitution.

In 1789, the U.S. Constitution was signed and put into effect. This action created an official government for the United States with a set of rules they would use to govern the country. It's the oldest written constitution still in use in the whole world.

Consider This

Why is it important for a country to have an official written constitution?

The Government's Beginnings

Before the U.S. government was formed, 13 American colonies had to first win their independence from Great Britain. The American Revolution lasted from 1775 to 1783. Once Americans won their independence, they had the huge task of making a whole new government.

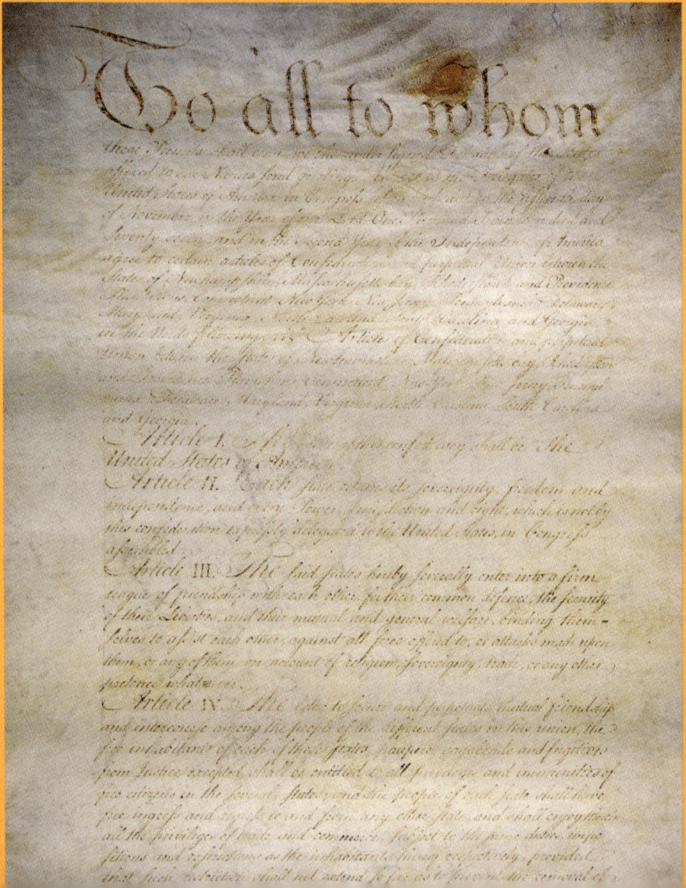

The first constitution of the United States was the Articles of Confederation, created in 1781. It had many issues.

The U.S. Constitution was signed at Independence Hall in Philadelphia, Pennsylvania.

In 1787, **representatives** from each of the states met in Philadelphia, Pennsylvania, to make a new Constitution. When they discussed the legislative branch, each state had its own concerns. Larger states had different issues than smaller ones. The smaller states wanted to be sure they had as much of a voice as the larger states. All of the states agreed to a system with two houses, one in which the number of representatives was based on population and one with an equal number of representatives per state.

WORD WISE

Representatives are people chosen to speak or act for others.

The Senate and the House

The agreement that created two houses of Congress was called the Great Compromise. It helped large and small states feel represented in Congress. In the Senate there are 100 senators, two from each state. Senators serve six-year terms. A term is the length of time a person holds an office. The people of each state elect their senators.

Every ten years, a census gathers basic information, such as how many people live in a state. That helps decide how many representatives that state should have.

People vote only for the representative from their district.

The House is made up of 435 representatives who serve two-year terms. States with bigger populations have more representatives than states with smaller populations. States that have more than one representative are divided into sections called districts. California, the most populated state, has the most representatives.

Consider This

How does the two-house system of Congress work for both large and small states?

Leaders of the Legislature

Each part of Congress has leaders with important roles. The House leader is called the speaker of the House. The **political party** that has the most members in the House is called the majority party. Members of that party get to vote for the speaker. The speaker's job is to oversee the meetings of the House.

Nancy Pelosi became the first female speaker of the House in 2007.

As vice president in a 50-50 Senate, Kamala Harris had to cast many tie-breaking votes.

The Senate leader is called the president of the Senate. The vice president of the United States serves as president of the Senate. However, the vice president votes only if there is a tie. Another senator, called the president pro tempore, leads the Senate when the vice president is absent. The president pro tempore is one of the senators. The president pro tempore is chosen by the majority party in the Senate.

WORD WISE

A political party is a group of people who usually have similar beliefs about the role of government and how it should be run.

The party with the fewest members in each house, called the minority party, also has leaders. This person is called the Senate minority leader or the House minority leader. This person speaks for his or her party and helps to decide what kind of projects or laws the party is going to work on. The minority leader may also be called the leader of the opposition. It is his or her job to make sure the ideas of the minority party are heard.

Both parties also have whips. A whip is the person who manages the members of each party. Whips make sure party members show up when there is a vote. They also work to make sure members vote on issues important to their party. Sometimes, members of both parties have a similar goal and vote the same way, which is called a bipartisan vote.

In 2023, Senator Charles Schumer, a Democrat, was the majority leader in the Senate.

compare and contrast

The Democrats and the Republicans are the two major political parties in the United States, and each has its own values. Why is this good for government?

Mitch McConnell, a Republican, is the longest-serving party leader in the Senate.

The Power to Make Laws

The U.S. Constitution gives Congress the power to create laws. Each new law starts out as a document called a bill. For a bill to become a law, a member of the House or Senate must introduce it. Then the bill goes to committee. This is a small group of senators or representatives who review the bill.

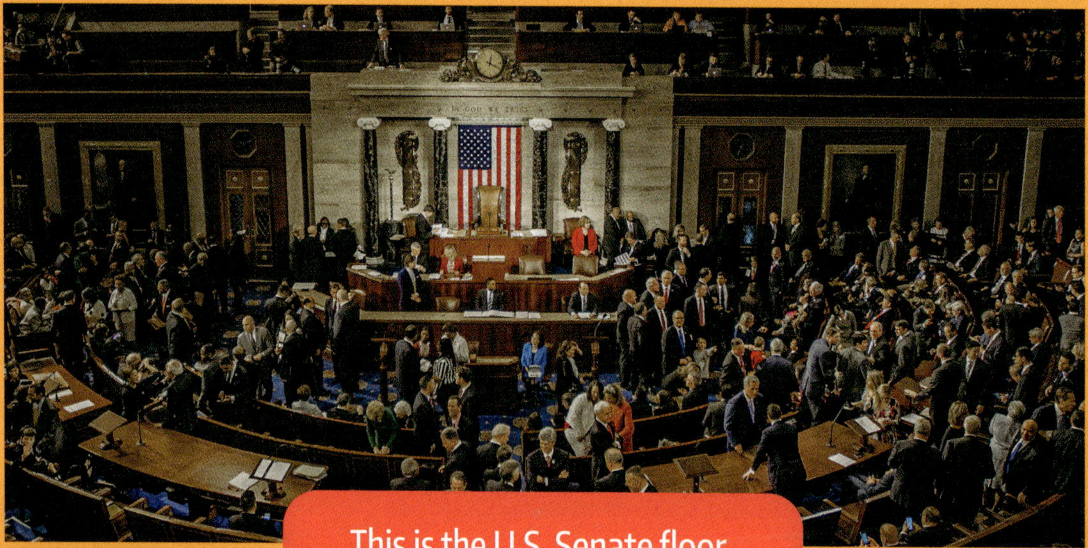

This is the U.S. Senate floor, where senators vote on bills.

This is the U.S. House chamber, where House representatives vote on bills.

Once the bill is ready, it is sent to the full House or Senate. House and Senate members debate, or talk about, the bill. Then they vote to pass or reject the bill. If more than half of each house's members approve the bill, it then goes to the other house for a vote. To become a law, both houses must pass a bill. Then, it's on to the White House.

Consider This

It takes many steps for a bill to become a law. Why are these steps important?

The president is the next person to see a bill once it passes both houses. If the president signs the bill, it becomes a law. The president can veto, or reject, a bill. A vetoed bill can still become a law, however. This happens if two-thirds of both houses vote to override, or undo, the veto.

The Supreme Court is the highest court in the country.

The president decides if bills become laws or not. This picture shows President Joe Biden signing a bill into law.

If people think there is a problem with a law, they may ask the Supreme Court to review the law. The court may decide that the law **violates** the U.S. Constitution. In that case, the law is no longer in force. This ensures Congress doesn't create laws that are not in the best interests of the people. It's another way to keep one branch from getting too powerful.

WORD WISE

To violate means to break or fail to observe a rule.

The Power to Declare War

Sometimes it becomes necessary for the United States to defend itself or its people. The president may ask Congress to declare war. In that case, Congress alone has the power to declare war. This power is called the War Powers Clause.

The president can send troops to handle different situations that require the military if it is necessary, which is not an act of war.

The last time Congress voted to formally declare war was during World War II in 1941.

For Congress to declare war, the president must ask Congress to vote on whether the government should or should not declare war on another country. Two-thirds of both the Senate and the House must vote in favor of declaring war. Congress has formally declared war on only a few occasions: the War of 1812, the Mexican-American War, the Spanish-American War, World War I, and World War II. Declaring war is not something to be taken lightly.

Consider This

Only five wars have been declared by Congress in U.S. history. Why might that be?

The Power to Collect and Manage Money

The government needs money to pay for all the programs that keep the country running. It pays for these things through taxes. Congress has the power to create and collect taxes. The money collected from taxes is used to help the United States in many ways.

A large portion of U.S. spending is for defending the country.

Have you ever visited a National Park? These are run by the federal government.

Taxes are used for construction projects on roads and public buildings. Social programs like medical care, education, and Social Security are also supported by taxes. Tax money is also used to support the people who serve in the military. It is used to buy equipment and weapons for the troops. Taxes are also used to help run the national parks and programs in the arts. If the government doesn't have enough money for everything it needs, it can borrow money.

Consider This

Taxes must be paid by every citizen and business. How does that benefit the country?

Bonds are one solution that help the government raise more money. Bonds are like loans between the government and the people who buy them. When people buy bonds, the government gets the money. The money must be paid back by a certain date. Some of the taxes that the government collects are used to pay back the money for the bonds. Congress decides how the money from the bonds is spent. Congress cannot raise money this way all the time. There is a limit to how much debt the government can have.

The Federal Reserve was founded in 1913 to make the American banking system as stable as possible.

People need to trust that banks will keep their money safe.

Congress created the Federal Reserve System to provide financial services—like a bank—to the U.S. government. It makes sure that the economy of the country is healthy. It also makes sure that money moves through the banking system smoothly. It's important that banks have enough money to lend people and cash checks or people wouldn't be able to trust that their money is safe.

Consider This

Why is it important to the stability of the nation to have a healthy economy?

The Power to Regulate Trade

Regulating trade, or the exchange of goods and services, with other countries is another power of Congress. Congress manages trade by deciding on what can and cannot come into the United States. They can also put taxes on imports—the goods that are brought in. The taxes may make the goods more expensive to buy than American-made products. This may make it more likely that people will buy American-made products instead of ones from other countries.

You can tell where a product was made by looking at the tag.

Imported goods often travel on huge cargo ships.

The government may also stop trading with another country for economic or political reasons. For example, Congress may not want to trade with a country whose government is doing something that the United States disagrees with. Ending or limiting trade with another country is called trade sanctions.

Consider This

What kinds of goods are imported from other countries? Why?

A Powerful Congress

Many people think only of lawmaking when they think of Congress's powers. But it has other powers too. Congress can coin, or make, money. It can give patents and copyrights for new ideas. A patent or copyright makes sure that a person or business cannot steal an idea from another person or business.

People from other countries may become U.S. citizens through naturalization.

The U.S. Post Office has a big job. They deliver cards between friends, important documents, and even voting ballots.

Congress sets the rules for naturalization, or the process for people from other countries to become U.S. citizens. Congress is also in charge of mail delivery. The U.S. Post Office makes sure mail makes it across the country and decides the days of the week that mail is delivered.

Congress can **impeach** the president or other officials if they may have broken the law. This ensures that no government official grows so powerful that they're above the law. With all these powers, Congress is a valuable part of the U.S. government.

WORD WISE

Impeach means to charge someone with misconduct.

Glossary

colonies: Counties or areas under the control of another country.
committee: A smaller group that works in support of a larger group.
debate: To discuss an issue to understand both sides.
district: An area of land overseen by a local government.
document: A written representation of one's thoughts or ideas.
federal: Relating to the national level of government.
financial: Having to do with money.
govern: To rule over.
import: To bring goods into a country from someplace else for sale.
judicial: Relating to the court system.
majority: More than half of the total.
military: The armed forces, including the army, air force, navy, and marines.
minority: Less than half of the total.
misconduct: Unacceptable behavior.
patent: A legal protection to someone who has an idea or invention.
regulate: To adjust the amount, rate, or speed of something.
term: A fixed or limited period of time.
veto: To reject a decision made by a law-making body.

For More Information

Books

Abramson, Jill. *What Is Congress?* New York, NY: Penguin Workshop, 2021.

McDaniel, Melissa. *The U.S. Congress.* New York, NY: Children's Press, 2020.

Stratton, Connor. *Congress.* Lake Elmo, MN: Focus Readers, 2024.

Websites

Around the Capitol
kids-clerk.house.gov/grade-school/lesson.html?intID=33
Go on a tour of the U.S. Capitol Building with this helpful government website.

Legislative Branch: Congress
www.ducksters.com/history/us_legislative_branch.php
Explore more about the legislative branch and its powers.

Three Branches of Government
kids.nationalgeographic.com/history/article/three-branches-of-government
Learn more fun facts about the three branches of the U.S. government.

Index